GRASSHOPPER

Helen Hawley

Turnstone Press

copyright © 1984 Helen Hawley

Turnstone Press
603-99 King Street
Winnipeg, Manitoba
Canada

Printed in Canada.

Canadian Cataloguing in Publication Data

Hawley, Helen, 1937-
  Grasshopper

A poem.
ISBN 0-88801-090-7

I. Title.
PS8565.A94G7 1984   C811'.54   C85-091016-1
PR9199.3.H38G7 1984

A wise man may grasp how ghastly it shall be
when all this world's wealth standeth waste,
even as now, in many places, over the earth
walls stand, wind beaten
hung with hoar-frost; ruined habitations.

(from *The Wanderer*)

PART ONE

Prairie floods out on all sides
wind billows grass . . . . and that's all
between Moose Jaw and Medicine Hat
no trees not even (maybe) farms   just surge of grass
and the inevitable telephonepole line   alongside it
rolls up one inclination
and down into a trough
up towards the next crest   and down again
an endless sequence of beginnings

Hop

beginnings or movements suggest hope
and I am immobilized behind green-tinted glass
belting down the Trans Can in a Greyhound bus
a ninety-miles-an-hour wonder bus
that bisects all that grass

I wanted to stand in long grass
watch it flow from my centred feet out
in all directions

or walk through grass and take the centre with me

not by myself not before or after Jennifer
my best friend in high school or Steve   my cousin   Pat
who used to sit on drifts with me
in crystal winter nights and hear how
Knox church bells could slice the coldest stars
four miles away
hear midges shrill through wild wheat
through the listening ears of Ken
when I had found the half-drowned pup in the creek
promised he'd help me bring it up Aunt Joan
not by myself but with she used to like to walk with me
and talk about the family
and show how meadowlarks leap out of prairie roses
                                        not by myself
not bold but bent in the same direction
when a sudden grass wind makes patterns on our skins
but everyone owns cars these days
hoping to embrace my people again I can only drive
                                        through them

5

I was born near here   Swift Current   why now
do I speed/split my birthright hills/hope
in this bus enthralled?   why did I go away so
for so long: "that's all" is everything!   to go
so far   for so long means   I may never return again
may never again bear blood
through all that waiting grass

                              out there

Seas of grass   that
run in such questing winds
to round horizons out of sight

Forfeit
forfeit of birthright   for such long absences
Why go?

The old woman loved to sing   every morning
from the balcony of her Saskatoon apartment   she
joined the dawn chorus of birds

                                        but the chirrup, chirrup
of her voice was too much for the neighbours
they called the cops   took her to court   "It's like
she was mourning the dead"   they said   "we . . .
can't stand it"

Too long away though my bones still rock near Anteloup
Bull Skull is my signpost and I hop
a bit west or east of here for home

Tourist now I am among the names of Muskrat Creek
                                        and Balmalea
feet chatter near the Rush Lake detour but I cross
behind the green glass with no fields or face

Beat of my blood is all around me as I am driven through
grass just out of reach along the bus route
and the juice and airs of home removed from me

Grasshopper
you tour the prairie around
bearing no fields and no footprints with you
to record your various names.

not even as Tourist can be   birthplace touched
the glass is always between   death's dark green intervention
deceives the bounding fields
out there . . . . . or maybe   not as tourist
but as sole Survivor
visited this place?

how we long to talk to each other   how we
reach out and we slip
past each other on a different track   you
locked in your bus and I locked in mine
passing each other on empty prairie roads

Hop

hoping to embrace my people again I can only
drive past them
maybe it's not Grasshopper's business
to be there anyway

It's an earthstepper's werth
to wander all over is fixed

Birth-place marks the start
but from then on   birth-space is denied
and today time doesn't matter
since there's no longer home
office to come home from
or deadline to catch

Maybe through wandering I have even pawned my name

Nameless I am   a non-person now
in my own eyes   as in the eyes
of my former families

Freak.   Earthstepper.

A friend tried to help   showed me the Other Regina
the City behind the City   one-storey-frame-houses   cheap
peeled paint   the dog who
barked down silence   the Street-
With- No- Name   empty warehouses
flanked the origins of railway tracks
that sank into weeds not sixty yards away
grain elevator under a spell as junk depot
deserted now   about to crumble
                    prairie crowded the edges of yards
crept along tracks
took over vacant lots   it was wild and flowing
and the sun blazed all around the ruins
but no people walked there   my friend said
beware of anyone
we might be lucky enough to see "They're only ghosts in here"
he explained

Grasshopper
you will not find your old footprints in that
little prairie city nearly on the roads lost
in the middle of those running plains

How can you   Earthstepper   survive those signs?
wind hits the glass from the other side and
you will not find your old footsteps on this nameless road

PART TWO

through holes in the road   smell smell the sour earth

through cracks in walls of apartment blocks see see the
incandescent desires orange shivers in
a drear dun room when the door was shut
finally against all expectation

when blocks were first set up people didn't realise
that there would be no transfer

if we shattered them to bits then could we not
rebuild them in a way that moulded them more closely
to our wanting skins?

leaking ceiling   rain falls through roof onto the rented tv set
newspapers cover it to try to keep it dry

nobody ever turns up when the emergency service is called

look at Mr Livingstone   his body lay
on his bathroom floor for five months and a day
before it was discovered

in the eyes of the man who lives across the landing
also alone in four small rooms the same
questions crease his dreams and desecrate his name

his door's the same
as door next door and miles of corridors repeat
each terror's vandalism   just outside identical
but separated rooms

staircases cannot
lead upwards   or   downwards
                          or inside
no sirens   nothing

"if I ever had a real job you'd see my dust!"
"I've worked hard for more than forty years and
what's it got me?   nothing"
"We loved the kid from his first marriage just like
our own   what went wrong?   i   just
                                        don't
                                                understand"
"maybe at six a m they'll kick down my door
haul me out of bed well   it's a deliverance of sorts"
"not much fun being on the dole   no place to go
no one to be   no name   nothing
i'm waiting"   "but Ron went
from his bungalow and carefully planned garden straight
through U of H to study how koalas mate   why
did he try to kill himself?   all I remember is
his wistful eyes that stared and stared month after day all day
out of its big front window"
"I remember too how buffalo blacked plains
just here near Swift Current not more than ninety years ago
and how we had to sell the bones for food"
"I farmed here since I emigrated if I had to do it again
not worth the sweat"

Burnt wrecks of many cars dead   whenever homes
                                        wrecked
vacated become
                complete destruction might be just the thing
                    bring sanity
                            to all these emptied spaces?
                                No.

No Emergency Service.

I came back to be with you again
Cheryl in your yellow clapboard house
beside the railway tracks
Mike we used to play baseball together in grade five
but now you boss the Last Chance Cafe
I came back to briefly be with you   brother
who seeks gold gophers beyond Eleventh Avenue
I came back to walk on the prairie with you Ann
to recall how we were defined on that country road
the one that turned past the last houses
                    near Smith's Market Garden
out to cryptic fields as wide as continents
under the whine of wind in the ditch grass
listen together to our pivotal voices seeping across the plains
Aunt Fox   Maggy who still whirled through suns

All around the switchgrass blows
and fields flow along the way
as far out as the edge of day
we roll the roads up before us   caught
by the promises of dawn
in this year's sun-caper   dance
                                    whoop for a title

Great Plains: how did we call you?
what will we call you?   you slide
 from your one name to the next
 like coyote slips from skins
                    up in coulees
                    or down along streets
from one self to the next . . . . Saskatchewan
Fort Laramie   Mahopa   Burdett
The West   Dakota   Land of Hope and Next Year Country
most of North America
what are your other names?

We moved in that first brave step
across the Bering Straits   or
over the Atlantic and the East
bearing a new word
a new round of remembered words

Across what bridges
into which kindling plains
speaking whose tongues?

The West: you are not all of our darknesses

Alone I am
there is no laughter to greet
a returning grasshopper
but it's not from nuclear disaster

There are so many faces that green glass distorts
child images once focussed I moved
                              gapless
between gripped hands and the revolving grass
touched merry-go-round plains and knew
there could not be a break   now freak
                                          grasshopper
I am not even once removed
            my cupped flesh rushed up by this bus but not
            beyond its dark green windows so the whole round
            dissolves   and my own   walked-memory
                                             heard-memory
                                             heart-memory
            holds apart   hello! Hello!   the greeting smiles not
not!   not!!   so terrible a break
between grins such a reaching out
out that could mean only just beyond dark glass or spin
like flywheel out to orbit

to close it all again?

Idea of a Desecrated City as a Deserted Threshold

Not even rubble mars the utter desolation of this country road
no stone shifts   no grain of dust breathes
implications of greening earth
across this hollowed sky   the storm clouds blown
Sun switches on
a lintel leaps from a scream and the rectangle beneath it
once door or window   frames a withered field
  Out through such tottering pledges were all people led
  into such absences of leaf
  that business deals rescinded   grains roared fire   governments
  winced of course   firms aimed over the winds
  and fell into Nevada   dust
  we nearly on the roads grew shadows   and our shadows
  struck us back   so in the end
  only our silhouettes held gentian clamours
  on a burnt-out threshold   once there was Mr Bates
  who left to thresh that time   here were his daughters and his son
  playing hop-scotch in such ordinary porches
  Mrs Thomas once
  belonged to say she would be home
  after she'd had her apprehensions drawn
  at the Regina clinic

Fallen bones
will not mar this step to undone roads or fields
nor will any absence of a cry
beat down into these silences

but it's not from nuclear disaster

Idea of a Desecrated City as an Empty Road

Shout
the empty road is as fugitive
as your inability
                    Grasshopper
to account for your passage through

there are no names to show it   .

"hello hello   I've been expecting you
for a hundred years or more"

there are no sounds of screeching tyres
no urgent knocking on doors   replies
to calls   No Emergency Service

"We are concerned about the violations
                    and the rage and rape
directed against us"   "All decisions
have to be objective probably not submitted
to the majority of watchers wanderers
                    aren't we all wanderers   all of us . . .

Fragments From the Song of Fools

After Empedocles had named the wonders
Earth and Water, Fire and Air
and told how Strife would knock asunder
all that from each mixing Weather
Love had glued together
he threw himself into the crater too
there are no Afterspeakers there

                    * * *

The greater the Power, the greater the Folly
the Songs of the Strivers are mighty and jolly
Who listens to each Vow or Lay
Lives like a Fool 'til Earth blows away

                    * * *

Isolation does not bring relief from the Absurd
a Tourist in a Ruined Home is seldom heard

                    * * *

That the machines had taken over was insignificant
I am still not afraid of those greenglass buses
boundering these quiet fields
I could walk right up to the reddest combine fears
digital remains will never impress me

the absence of the children is the worst terror

"But we must maintain that terror. It is the deterrent
that has kept the peace for thirty-nine years."

In the middle of that silence
is a deeper silence   fields settle
earth-forming reverses   dust drops
next is the un-leafing of the world
the un-extending of the world
the un-solidifying of the world
the un-quaking of the world
the un-taking-form of the world
          only the void of the world
          which the Source-of-Night has fled

the West is no more

The Sun Beat Down

The field is a memory of a round horizon
bisected by a road
full of locked buses
the city is a road
full of locked buses with green-darkened windows
full of the echoes of our fury
FULL OF THE ECHOES OF OUR FURY
and the latest broadcast winding down
on transistor radios

And we go
past fields no longer newsworthy
beyond split thresholds
on roads that broke the circle

where there is no circle any more around us

The Sun Beat Down

dissolving circles

the sun beat down   honey   over all
the sun beat down
the suns   Oh the sun   Oh the suns is
a brighter blast of black or white could not outlive
such emptiness of road   the road
the rubble   no road
all roads gone
all is gone   honey
                    all is nothing

Idea of a Desecrated City as a Withered Field

It's not a bare field
that will keep us from falling in
rather our reason inverts what we really know
so that we forget what we were looking for
rounds of families in seasoned plains
reduce to metaphors   or search for rings
                    we're reminded
whenever mist encircles field
that we're named at the centre of that circle
we in the centre of it all
the completed meaning of that growing field
grass sprouting from us all round towards the mist
through mist
to an unbroken circle just beyond the mist
hint of pure white elders
or other faces
withered field
may only contain an intention
is not whole in itself
an intention that flickers like a half-glimpsed path
from one edge of a misunderstanding
across
to the other edge

I will describe my grass faces
how they contour the plains   make the earth round
hold fast from wrecked thresholds
complete the circle again

seas of grass
bend in the winds of our urgent leaps
trace where we long to reach to horizons out of sight

PART THREE

Prairie Haiku

They didn't need to kill my Jack when they took the money
he would have given it to them
he wasn't any hero

The house costs ninety thousand and it's only three years old
but there are gaps between the windows and the walls
the basement's sinking

So what if sulphur wastes from my factory run into the lake
nobody lives in these parts at all
only a few Indians

The bracket clock's just darling and it's only
                                four hundred dollars
I must have the enamelled candlesticks as well
to go with my Mauch vase   ·

I'm scared to walk those three blocks from the bus stop
                                to your house
after dark   men in cars cruise right beside me
they get out and chase me

We've got two cars and two phones and three television sets
and a computerised purple dishwasher that sings
but it's not as good as Blain's

Catfish Joe's in jail again but he didn't do anythng
he got eighteen months for sassing a cop
he wasn't even drunk

43

I have been too long away   my prairie is not so old
but older than this

                                        mindweary
from hesitating alone elsewhere in too-old-too-
cramped-streets; surrounded again by these
    dimmed fields hinting rounds now   i have
    come back only to pass through   again though
    a grasshopper may jump seas   I may never
    encompass   Earthstepper I
        I could have walked for years over these surging
plains because there i was born believing that
I was once more contained in the centre of their
            charmed horizons between Moose Jaw and
      Medicine Hat I could have
talked   I cannot even   hear I
                                        could have talked to
            all those voices still concerned
behind thin telephone wires
                        but there was only time to say how
are you   what
are the children   doing?

The earthworks crumble   their titles lie
stripped of laughter   held sere
beside locked doors   wars shook off several
most honourable names   some victims of car crashes slid
over the highway   one was smothered as a babe
by his mother who could not stand his screams   one by
cancer forced to die and by hollow-eyed brother Bob
buried   everyone is not
felled by nuclear terror   some holocausts are found
every day among our common thresholds

A city in normal times is always so blasted

where is Suzanne these days? Why doesn't Eddy ever write?
you'd think he didn't care

Barry has his nose forever in his work   no time
for anybody else   look at his family wife left him
fled to Alagoinhas in Brazil two sons in jail for larceny and Sue
who walks the streets   for nights   who
and who cares

the deaths of all my families
arrived at different times with different hungers help
       Winyanketehca
       Shoveller
       or Jane MacVie or Tom Hunt or other help
help   and no one comes   nor cares
flat circle could be moonplain not seed not god
good for anything (but synonymous with greed)

We wanted fair land   a delight of plain
where blossoms of every colour lifted
to brighten the air   where lasting song
was season's rondel of praise   there would be
gold cloth of cattle mantling earth
silver cloth of geese embroidering skies
there would not be any greed   treachery
or harsh voices would not turn us from each other
no one would stand higher to make smaller
we would all dance together in the best of sweet grass
circled by pure white elders
across the shining prairie
this is what we thought we were looking for

West desecrated
                    Grasshopper roams
the several deaths of those dear at home shunt
                              Grasshopper away

it's an old flight across seas to call cares
among unheeding ears meanwhile back on the plains
things go on much as they did before

when the wanderer
longing to rediscover round memories of Jim and Mom
and Sarah Jane and Avonlea or fields a once-remembered
wholeness   returns to flicker momentarily
on that same prairie   only can
be rushed through landscape as a tourist on a bus

highly sophisticated technology does not lead to
any jubilee
Big Time machines do not run to Better Bonding

Oh that bare prairie!
Oh the smallness of our moments   the hugeness of its plains
it mocks us on our roads   then swears to let us free
its sense of past and now   of tears and ecstacy
pours from the promised fields and recalls each transient name

First in that radient sweep there's a sense of daze and dread
vast isolation swells   divides me from my fellow souls
then from a racking haze deep compassion wells and rolls
for faces not yet born and for faces long since dead

Then there's a lightness in my head and a losing sense of pain
then prairie resolves outward and I see the coyotes pass
and mirrored in my meagre years like images on glass
flying fragments of my people that will not whoop again

And I'm a speck in dust in that outward rushing will
a grasshopper who's wierded to call the roads alone
yet even as I'm driven through my broken prairie home
held at the storm's round eye   that being eye of still

I gambolled across the continental field
the surrendered metaphors of sea
I called from a clue of wholeness
whenever mists rolled the horizon nearer
or when its eye chose to jump through masks

And I carried the nub of that round grass

through Ed who waited underneath the streetlight
through Joe who could not go
because he did not have a home to come from
through Winiford who had not dawdled but had gone straight
          on through school

through Darlene   the darling of the town . . . whose smiles
were as wide as the canyons she had to walk through
her eyes were as deep   (they were as deep)
as the discarded pledge of big bluestem
that once had brought them all to light

through Gene who was the neatest   shelving stray thirsts
through Abe who was first to raise his pigs here back
                                    in ninety-three
through Jinny who loved her aunt the best

through Jake who was the toughest   loudest   quickest
because he was so small inside his fist

and Little Mo the most forgotten of them all

through Missus Preiss once a middling bloom
but wilted since her thousand days
bent over the stove to feed nine mouths
on half a forkful of grit

through Mister Bradshaw who was once a soldier
until a brighter flower struck his gut
now he is watchman at the Purley Works

through Beverley who fought back
and her sister Mae who didn't

through Dan who would not leave his Mom
wet his bed at nights but dreamed
in colours no one else had ever seen

through Gibbs who made nothing but money

through the baby nobody knew

through Eileen eight and frightened to look at Mister Dix
next door in case she saw his tawny eyes
begin to whizz again   his yellow thumbs
reach out to grab her

through Pete and Lupe and Once a Minute Ben
and old hawk warrior Jeanette
on the sunporch of her Crane Hills shack
surrounded by the sweating grass and singing about rain

through each dear asking face
wherever I went from there
and even my return behind dark glass
could not alter that
                     place circles
face circles
can be recalled in transit even across the disguised grass
even the lost postulations for the Last Best West
can be called back again